KING EDWARD VI

A Life from Beginning to End

Copyright © 2019 by Hourly History.

Table of Contents

Introduction

Edward VI, the only legitimate son of the infamous Henry VIII, became England's first genuinely Protestant monarch at the mere age of nine. He was too young to rule of his own accord, but the regency that was appointed for Edward allowed him to continue the work of his father with regards to religious reform. England saw Henry VIII sever the tie between the Roman Catholic Church and the Church of England. It was Edward, however, who initiated the true reformation of religion in England by renouncing Catholic ceremonies and rituals. The Church of England became a truly Protestant entity during the reign of Edward VI.

At this time, Tudor England was facing major instability in many areas. The economy was failing because of an expensive war, and divides among the English people led to serious unrest. Two years into his reign, Edward lost control over his opposers, and the kingdom was engulfed by riots and rebellions.

A devout Protestant, Edward remained focused on what he believed was the most important issue during his time on the throne: religion. The young king did not want England to fall back into line with the Roman Catholic Church, so during his reign many laws were established to govern the future of religion in his country. Edward also made sure to establish a line of succession that would not threaten his religious reformation should he pass away. These efforts would be in vain, however, as his Catholic half-sister Mary would claw her way to the throne upon the king's death.

Edward VI's place in history was brief indeed, but his reign would have long-term impact on the religious practices of the English people. Edward was the first monarch of England whose life was centered around Protestantism from beginning to end.

Chapter One

Born in a Time of Unrest

"A Prince, conceived in most lawful matrimony between my Lord the King's Majesty and us."

—Jane Seymour

Edward Tudor was born on October 12, 1537, at Hampton Court Palace to King Henry VIII and his third wife, Jane Seymour. Before Edward's birth, Henry had one son who was born out of wedlock, which meant that Edward was the first legitimate male heir to the English throne. Henry was overjoyed at the birth of his much-awaited baby boy. The parents had Edward christened three days later, and he was given the titles of earl of Chester and duke of Cornwall. His half-sister Mary, who was at this point considered an illegitimate daughter of Henry's because of the annulment of his marriage to Mary's mother, was named as godmother. Unfortunately, Henry's joy would become somewhat overshadowed by the death of Edward's mother, who would remain Henry's favorite out of the six wives he would have during his life.

Jane gave birth to Edward in her room after three long nights of labor but was thought to be healthy after the delivery. Reveling in the afterglow of having produced the male heir her husband had been longing for, she appeared to recover fast and was quick to write letters to friends and family announcing the birth of the prince. But less than two weeks after Edward's birth, Jane fell ill. The sickness came on quickly, and she died the night after the symptoms presented themselves. Most likely, some form of postnatal infection was responsible for taking the life of the queen.

Even though Henry VIII regretted the loss of his young wife, he could not help but feel relieved and overjoyed that he had finally solved his "great matter" of securing the line of succession. Doted on and adored by his father, Edward proved to be healthy from the start of his life. Henry was known to hold the baby boy every day, often standing at the window so the people of England could get a glimpse of the future king.

The baby boy's life was of the utmost importance. Henry's other children, who he had at this point disowned and considered illegitimate, were girls. At this time in England, there was no precedent for a female monarch to rule in her own right. Edward was not just Henry's only legitimate son—he was the only male heir of the Tudor family for that whole generation. For those reasons, it was feared that if Edward died, so too would the Tudor dynasty on the English throne.

Fortunately, Edward grew quickly. Other than poor eyesight and occasional illnesses (including a life-threating bout of quartan fever at age four), he was a robust, healthy little boy. In his early years, he was known to be both athletically and intellectually inclined. The king wanted to make sure that Edward stayed in the best health possible and made it very clear that his son's quarters were to be kept extremely clean at all times and he was to always be in very secure environments. After having waited so long to have a male heir to the throne, it seemed Henry was not willing to take any risks when it came to his son's wellbeing. Extra precaution was to be taken at all times.

During Edward's first years, he was raised by women of his household. At age six, he began his formal education, receiving tuition from the best tutors available to the court. Studious and intelligent, Edward was an easy child to teach. He was well-rounded in his talents and participated in athletics, learned liberal sciences, excelled at geometry, and played instruments. The subjects he was taught included Latin, French, Greek, and theology.

Edward was the first English monarch to be raised as Protestant, and his teachings surrounding religion were skewed toward religious reform. But even though he was Protestant, he attended mass and held relics of the saints in reverence; later he would let go of those practices, even going as far as making it unlawful to observe traditional Catholic acts of worship. It was his father's last wife, Catherine Parr, who really lit Edward's Protestant fire. She became the mother figure in Edward's life and influenced him with her steadfast Protestant faith.

When he was a child, Edward and his half-sisters Mary and Elizabeth got along quite well. The young prince even once wrote to Mary exclaiming, "I love you most." That would be a far cry from what would become of the siblings later in life. The religious differences between Mary, who was a devout Catholic, and Edward would prove too much to foster a lasting relationship. Elizabeth, however, managed to stay on friendly terms with both her siblings during most of her life. Her Protestant faith and the fact that she was only four years older than Edward made it easy for the prince and her to connect. Even Mary, who was twenty years older than her siblings, formed a close bond with Elizabeth, perhaps because of the similarities in how Henry VIII had treated their mothers (Mary's mother had been banished, eventually dying without being allowed to see her daughter, while Elizabeth's mother had been executed on dubious grounds).

Like Elizabeth, Edward did superiorly well in school. He paid much more attention to his studies than most other children did—perhaps because he wanted to be on par with Elizabeth, who was one of the most well-educated women of her generation. Edward lived quite the privileged life as the son of the king. Surrounded by the finest of home decorations and trimmings, the prince was raised with everything he could have wanted. His clothes were made of the finest materials and were even encrusted with gold and precious gems, as were his other possessions. Portraits of the boy show him standing in the fashion of his father, with a golden dagger that had jewels on the handle.

Visitors who came to see the king often brought Edward toys and other luxurious gifts. He was even given his very own troupe of entertainers. Some would say that Edward grew up a very spoiled child.

Chapter Two

The Rough Wooing

"This whole realm's most precious jewel."

—Henry VIII, describing his son

England's relationship with Scotland had been troublesome for quite some time. It was Henry's desire to bring unity between the two realms; of course, what he truly wanted was to gain some control of his own over Scotland, which he tried to do by using his son as a bargaining chip.

In 1543, when Edward was six years old, Henry signed the Treaty of Greenwich with the Scots. The agreement, also known as the Union of the Crowns, established peace between the two kingdoms. A second part of the treaty stipulated that Edward and Mary, Queen of Scots, who was only seven months old at the time, would be betrothed to each other. Mary was to be accompanied by an English nobleman and his wife until she was ten years old in preparation for her wedding with Edward. At ten, she would then have to move to England and reside there permanently.

The treaty was signed on July 1, 1543 and ratified on August 25 by James Hamilton, the regent for the infant Queen Mary of Scotland. However, in December of that same year, the Scottish Parliament renounced the agreement. Rather than creating peace between the kingdoms, the Treaty of Greenwich ended up creating more conflict that lasted for the next eight years. This period of war between England and Scotland, which became known as the Rough Wooing, formed part of the Anglo-Scottish Wars that began in the early fourteenth century and ended in the late sixteenth century.

Henry's attempt to force the Scottish to agree to the marriage between his son and Mary would prove unsuccessful. Many Scots did not want to ally with England because of what they saw as English mistreatment and bullying—Henry's break with Rome also did not help matters as the Scottish people wanted to keep their Catholic religion. Instead, Scotland's rulers were interested in renewing their alliance with France. Because the English did not have a good existing relationship with the French, it would have been a huge conflict of interest for Scotland to align with England.

Furious at the Scots' rejection of the marriage proposal, Henry ordered Edward's uncle, Edward Seymour who was the earl of Hertford at the time, to launch an all-out attack on Scotland in May of 1544. That attack would be the beginning of a war that would last long into Edward's reign on the throne.

In January of 1547, Edward was given a gift for the new year. It consisted of portraits of his father and his wife at the time, Catherine Parr. Edward wrote to Henry and his stepmother to thank them for the presents. About three weeks later, the king, who had struggled with obesity and ill health for some time, died at age 55. Edward Seymour and Sir Anthony Browne arrived to take the prince to Enfield where his half-sister Elizabeth lived. There,

Edward and Elizabeth were told that their father had passed away. Edward was nine years old and was about to be named the king of England and Ireland.

Chapter Three

England's First Protestant King

"I will say with certain intention, that I will see my laws strictly obeyed, and those who break them shall be watched and denounced."

—Edward VI

On February 16, 1547, Henry VIII was buried next to his third wife, Jane Seymour, in a tomb at Windsor. The king had made his wishes clear that he wanted to be buried with the mother of his male heir, and those wishes were honored upon his death. Meanwhile, Edward had been taken to the Tower of London. Some ceremonious rituals took place at the tower, including the naming of Edward Seymour as the young king's lord protector. Because Edward was still legally a minor, Henry had appointed a council of 16 regents in his will that were to rule collectively in Edward's place until he came of age. Nevertheless, the group agreed to hand over most of the power to Seymour, who became the de facto ruler during the first years of Edward's reign.

On February 20, 1547, Edward VI was crowned at Westminster Abbey as the new king of England, succeeding his father. Because of his age, the ceremonies were shorter than usual. Additionally, the religious reformation that had been ongoing under Henry VIII's rule made some of the traditional rituals no longer applicable. Part of the coronation consisted of urgings from Archbishop Thomas Cranmer for Edward to continue working on the reformation started by his father. Cranmer had been a strong supporter of Henry's efforts to separate England from Rome, and he wanted to see the new king open the doors for Protestantism even more. The archbishop's efforts would prove fruitful.

Following Edward's coronation and Seymour's appointment as lord protector, substantial gifts of lands and titles were distributed amongst the council members. Seymour would, for example, style himself as the duke of Somerset from this point on. By March, Seymour was able to make decisions virtually as a monarch, having secured the right to do so by young King Edward. The lord protector could now name men to the council whenever he saw fit and had been permitted to consult the council only when he wanted to. Although Seymour was accepted in his position by most, there were a few men who opposed his rise to power.

Thomas Wriothesley, a chancellor known for being religiously conservative, disapproved of Seymour's almost total monarchical level of control. His objections did not go unnoticed. Soon enough, Wriothesley was ousted from his seat as chancellor on the premise that he had sold some of his offices to other delegates. The lord protector's own brother, Thomas Seymour, would also show opposition to his position of power. This opposing threat proved harder to get rid of as Thomas wanted some of the power for himself. He too was the king's uncle, so he did not see why he should not be afforded some of the same privileges his brother had been given.

In an effort to appease his brother, Seymour offered Thomas the title of baron, a seat in the council, and appointment to the lord admiralship. The bribes fell short. Thomas yearned for the same level of power his brother had been given; his ego would accept no less. Thomas resorted to scheming behind Seymour's back and trying to degrade him in the eyes of young King Edward. He told the boy that Seymour was depriving him of his power and retaining too much control over the money and other issues that fell under the protectorship. Edward, however, was firm in his belief of always asking the council for guidance as his father had left instructions for him to do.

Although Thomas's discussions with the king did not lead to Seymour's removal from power, he did manage to secure Edward's support for marrying Henry VIII's widow, Catherine Parr—a union which Seymour very much opposed. Their marriage in 1547 was seen by many as just another part of Thomas's ambitious plan to acquire power. After the wedding, Thomas would become part of a household that included both Elizabeth and Jane Grey (Henry VII's granddaughter), giving him unlimited access to two potential heirs to the throne.

About a year after the wedding, when Catherine was pregnant, it became clear that Thomas was actively pursuing an intimate relationship with Elizabeth, who was only 13 years old at the time. The king's half-sister was then removed from the household and sent away to live with a family friend. Her removal stopped the contact between the two for a short time. But when, in September of 1548, Catherine died shortly after childbirth, Thomas started writing to Elizabeth again, intending to marry her. Elizabeth, however, stuck to the rules like her brother and deferred to the council for their guidance on whether she should marry Thomas or not.

For the lord protector and the council, Thomas's increasingly bold attempts to take control of the royal family had become intolerable. In February 1549, he was indicted on numerous charges of treason. He was soon deemed guilty through an act of attainder, which negated the need of having an open trial. On March 20, 1549, Thomas Seymour was beheaded.

Amidst all of the turmoil with his brother, Edward Seymour had pressing matters to attend to on other fronts. The majority of his attention was put into the war with Scotland. Although he was known for his military prowess, Seymour had a lot to prove as the lord protector and leader of England's forces. Since negotiations with the Scots had failed with the Treaty of Greenwich, Seymour decided to try to unite the kingdoms through conquest instead of marriage. In September 1547, his Scottish campaign started well as his forces won a crushing victory at the Battle of Pinkie Cleugh. Seymour then set about securing English control in the region by building garrisons and forts.

However, as the years dragged on, it became clear that the cost of manning and maintaining the garrisons in Scotland was unsustainable for the English economy. The vision Seymour had of bringing the two kingdoms together through force was not going to be realized. Scotland had aligned themselves with England's opposer, France, who soon came to offer support in defense of their ally. At this point, Mary, Queen of Scots had even been betrothed to the French king's son, further solidifying the bond between the two countries. When the French attacked English-occupied Boulogne in August of 1549, Seymour and his forces had no other choice but to leave Scotland and try to negotiate a peace with France.

At home in England, the people were in upheaval. Between the religious reformation and the expensive war with Scotland and France, many commoners felt that their grievances were not being taken into consideration by the ruling class. The year of 1549 saw many violent uprisings break out. A few of them necessitated extensive military intervention.

Chapter Four

The Year of Rebellions

"You are fleeced by these landlords for their private benefit, and as well kept under by the public burdens of State wherein while the richer sort favour themselves, ye are gnawn to the very bones."

—Robert Kett

One of the largest religious revolts during Edward's reign, the Prayer Book Rebellion, took place mainly in Devon and Cornwall. These regions did not take lightly to the introduction of the *Book of Common Prayer*, which was written to educate the English on the theology encompassed by the English Reformation. Some traditionally Catholic regions, including Devon and Cornwall, were still highly opposed to Protestantism, and the people resented the religious reformation that was forced upon them. Understandably, they despised the *Book of Common Prayer*, which called for the banning of all traditional Catholic pilgrimages and processions. It also resulted in the removal of all Catholic symbols around the country by commissioners who were sent out by the council and Archbishop Cranmer.

In Cornwall, the man sent to take down the Catholic icons was William Body. The people of Cornwall, furious at what they saw as desecration of their religious shrines, decided to take action. In April of 1548, Body was murdered by two locals. From that point forward, public unrest would continue to spread.

Once the new prayer book was published and distributed to the public, not everyone adopted the new standards right away. As a result of the slow adoption of the book's practices, the Act of Uniformity was passed in January of 1549. The act made it illegal to use the traditional Catholic liturgical rites and aimed to make religious worship in England consistent with Edward's religious reforms.

However, in the village of Sampford Courtenay in Devon, churchgoers convinced their priest to conduct their service in the traditional manner that they had always been used to, rather than what was dictated in the *Book of Common Prayer*. At the very next service, justices showed up to force the priest to adopt the new prayer book's provisions. Their intervention did not go smoothly. One of the men who supported the change, William Hellyons, ended up dead in the altercation. He was stabbed with a pitchfork right outside the church doors.

In the areas of Cornwall and Devon, people had been suffering for years with the inflation of prices on goods, the enclosure of communal land, and now the attacks on their religion. The once-peaceful people of these regions were angry, and that anger was channeled into attacks on the enforcers of the new policies and the wealthy landowners who had continued to benefit from all of the changes in the country. Occurrences of noblemen holing themselves up inside castles for protection were commonplace during the Prayer Book Rebellion. At St. Michael's Mount, a group of gentlemen had shut themselves in hoping to escape the torment of the rebels who were seeking to hurt or kill them. The rebels lit trusses of hay on fire and smoked the refugee noblemen out of their hiding places. Eventually, the noblemen were forced to surrender. The army of Cornwall then marched into Devon and joined forces with the rebels there.

The rebels wanted their religion and practices left alone. They had a saying that exhibited their disgust at the changes that King Edward and his council were forcing upon them. The slogan said, "Kill all the gentlemen and we will have the Six Articles up again, and ceremonies as they were in King Henry's time." The Six Articles that the people were referring to came about because of the king's desire to have religious uniformity throughout the kingdom. During Henry VIII's reign, Parliament had argued over six doctrinal questions to decide whether they should practice newly adopted rituals or existing customs. In the end, it was decided to stick to the traditional (Catholic) way of doing things. However, Edward had since ascending to the throne repealed the Act of Six Articles—much to the chagrin of many of his Catholic subjects.

By the summer of 1549, the rebellion had grown so large that Seymour had to send military forces to the region to stop it. He appointed Lord John Russell as leader of an army that, in addition to English soldiers, consisted of troops from Germany and Italy. After a series of battles during the months of June to August, the uprising was finally quelled. Thousands of rebels had lost their lives.

Another serious revolt taking place at the same time was led by Robert Kett. Kett, one of the wealthiest farmers in Wymondham, decided to join protestors in his region to object the enclosure of land. Landowners used this method to take small tracts of common land and consolidate them into larger sections and farms. The land would then be fenced off from the public and given to the landowner. Enclosure of common land allowed wealthy lords to become wealthier and left poor farmers with nowhere to graze their animals. During the 1540s, England had increasingly been struggling with this agricultural crisis. The English people relied heavily on the land to sustain themselves. Peasants used communal land to grow food and graze their animals—with nowhere to do that, people were starving and falling further and further into hardship.

In July of 1549, an uprising against land enclosure began in Wymondham. There was an annual feast held there every July 6 in honor of St. Thomas Becket. Becket was one of the patron saints of Wymondham Abbey. Because Henry VIII had ordered that Thomas Becket be removed from the church calendar, the performance of the play and the celebration surrounding it was unlawful. The event was the kick-off of what would turn into Kett's Rebellion.

On the heels of the celebration, some of the participants went to two villages southwest of Wymondham. Their mission was to rip down the fences that had been put up to keep people away from what had once been common land. They started with a wealthy landowner in Hethersett, a lawyer named John Flowerdew. Flowerdew had played a large role in the closing of Wymondham Abbey in 1538, so the rebels decided to target him first. Flowerdew resorted to bargaining and bribery to get the attackers to leave his land

and enclosures alone. Instead, he convinced them to move on and attack the enclosures of Robert Kett.

The Kett family had lived in the area for hundreds of years. Kett had helped to save the parish church when Wymondham Abbey had been shut down, which explains why Flowerdew had it out for him. The rebels showed up at Kett's property to confront him and tear down his fences but were, to their surprise, met with the sympathetic ears of a man who was willing to help them with their cause, rather than fight against them. Although Kett, being a wealthy farmer, had benefitted greatly from the enclosure policy, he understood the rebels' frustration and agreed that enclosure of common land should be forbidden. Kett offered to join the rebels in an uprising against the government and even helped them to tear down his own fences that had been installed around his land. After that, Kett followed the rioters back to Hethersett and proceeded to help them take down Flowerdew's fences as well.

The people of the rebellion, now led by Kett, designated a meeting place at an oak tree that was between Hethersett and Norwich. That tree, known as Kett's Oak, stands to this day. The symbol of the oak tree would become associated with the rebellion, especially since another oak tree would mark the center of the more long-lasting rebel camp at Mousehold Heath. On July 12, 1549, Kett and his group made it to Mousehold Heath after facing some minor resistance. The location was perfect for their headquarters because they were perched above Norwich and could see the whole city from there. They would keep their base at Mousehold for the next six and a half weeks. St. Michael's Chapel became the center of the operation and Mount Surrey, which had been the house of the earl of Surrey until he was executed in 1547, became a prison for holding captors of the rebel army.

Kett ran his brigade in a very organized fashion with a council of representatives. He and his council members would meet under the Oak of Reformation in the center of the camp to lay out their plans of motion or issue warrants for arrests. As word got around about the camp and the rebel forces, more and more people came to join the revolt. There were people from all around the region and some even from Norwich. Eventually, the camp at Mousehold Heath had a larger population of people than Norwich itself. At the time, Norwich was the second largest city in all of England at around 12,000 people. Some of the city authorities, including Mayor Thomas Codd, were asked to join the council at Mousehold to negotiate a settlement and did end up accepting the invitation.

Kett and the council wrote a list of demands, which was sent to King Edward and his lord protector. On a physical front, the rebel army was tearing down every fence and hedge they could find, and though it was mentioned in the list of demands that they wanted the enclosure process to cease that was only one small piece of what they were seeking in their rebellion. Their grievances included many more wrongdoings perpetrated by the ruling elite against the working class, for example the practice of rack-renting and corruption.

During the time that negotiations were in process, a truce was called between the representatives. On July 21, however, the truce came to an end. Bartholomew Butler, a messenger from the king's council, brought news from

London. Escorted by Norwich authorities, he went to the rebel camp and delivered a message from the king, which formally established Kett and his gathered army as rebels in the eyes of the Crown. Butler relayed that everyone would be offered pardons if they were to disperse their ranks and return to their homes immediately. Kett refused to take the offer on the grounds that he, nor any of the others who had joined him, had committed any crime.

There were far too many rebels to arrest them all, so Butler had to retreat to Norwich with his escort and Mayor Codd. They had at least formally informed Kett that he and his supporters were considered rebels and that they could be arrested and brought up on charges going forward. Following the meeting, both sides of the conflict began preparations for the battle they could see coming.

Norwich had been a source of supplies for Kett and his men. But when the truce ended, the city's gates were closed, and the rebels were not granted access to food or other necessities. Kett was unsure of what to do. There were far too many people to disperse them back to their homes, and Kett had not achieved what he set out to do. He felt that his only option was to attack Norwich.

On the same night the truce ended, Kett's army opened fire on the city of Norwich. Norwich responded with their own artillery. Bombardments from both sides continued throughout the night. In the morning Kett called off the artillery. He feared they were losing the battle so far and that the accuracy of the city defenses was going to deprive his army of all of their guns. Kett regrouped and, while waving a white flag, requested to be granted access back into the city. The officials of Norwich denied the request and kept the city gates closed.

In response, Kett had his artillery moved further up the hill and ordered his men to take aim at the city again. Norwich's guns could not reach the new location of the rebels' artillery, and Kett ordered a full-blown assault on Norwich once he saw that the rebels had the upper hand. His men charged full speed down the hill and across the river. They were met with arrow attacks, but it was not enough to stop the rebels from infiltrating the city. The army of rebels, under Kett's leadership, took over the city of Norwich on July 22, 1549.

At this point, King Edward ordered William Parr, the marquess of Northampton, to go to Norwich with 1,500 men to suppress the rebels. When the royal army got close to the city, a herald was sent in to demand a surrender. The mayor informed the herald that Kett and the rebels had left the city and retreated to their camp at Mousehold. The withdrawal from Norwich was part of Kett's plan. He had seen how hard it had been for the Norwich army to defend their city and decided it would be better to let Parr have his shot at defending against the same kind of attack the rebels had already successfully carried out.

Once in the city, the royal army prepared their defenses and assigned men to watch the streets. On July 31, an alarm was sounded in the middle of the night. Parr was alerted that the rebels were sneaking up on the patrolling soldiers and taking them out in the dark. The royal army then bolstered their defense on the most vulnerable side of the city which temporarily deterred further attacks. Just after breakfast on August 1, Parr was told that the rebels wanted to negotiate their surrender at Pockthorpe gate. However, upon arriving at the meeting place, no rebels were present. Instead, a large number of rebels were crossing the river to launch a surprise attack on the royal army. Realizing that his men were being overrun, Parr ordered a full retreat and left Norwich.

But even though this battle had been lost, the English Crown would not accept defeat. Edward and his government immediately sent another, even larger, army to end the rebellion at Norwich once and for all. John Dudley, the earl of Warwick, was entrusted with the responsibility to lead the almost 14,000 men who were going to take down Kett's army. When he attacked Norwich on August 24, the rebels were forced to retreat, but as they left they set fire to houses in an attempt to slow down their enemy. Standing up for what they believed was right, the rebels were not going to give up without a fight, and they even managed to seize some artillery meant for the royal army from a supply train.

After several days of skirmishes, Dudley finally defeated Kett in the Battle of Dussindale. The fighting, which took place in an open area, showcased the royal army's military superiority against what was mainly farmers and peasants. Kett quickly lost thousands of men; those who were not killed started to run. After the battle, captured rebels were hung at the Oak of Reformation. The royal army found Kett the night after the battle and brought him to the Tower of London. In December, he was found guilty of treason and was hanged at Norwich Castle. His brother William, who had also been part of the rebel army, was hanged on the same day at Wymondham Abbey.

Chapter Five

Struggling for Power

"The Duke of Somerset had his head cut off upon Tower Hill between eight and nine in the morning."

—Edward VI

By mid-1549, Lord Protector Edward Seymour had seen a steep decline in his popularity both among the English gentry and the government. The widespread social unrest and subsequent rebellions fell squarely on Seymour's shoulders because of his role as the king's acting regent. In October, the lord protector was made aware that the council was planning his imminent removal from power. In response, he brought the king to Windsor Castle, presumably for his own and the king's safety in the event of a coup, and issued a proclamation ordering all loyal troops to prepare to defend the land. Meanwhile, the council was laying out in writing all of the things Seymour had done wrong or incompetently as the protector to the king. The council then issued their publication, which also included the fact that the will of Henry VIII did not give Seymour any power—it was the council that had granted him authority.

Only about a week after Seymour had retreated with the king to Windsor Castle, he was arrested. At this point, he had realized that he lacked the support to take on his opposers and so he agreed to negotiate a settlement. Seymour was brought to the Tower of London where he faced several charges; King Edward wrote in his diary that they included "ambition, vainglory, entering into rash wars in mine youth, negligent looking on Newhaven, enriching himself of my treasure, following his own opinion, and doing all by his own authority." However, Seymour would eventually be released from the tower, cleared of all charges, and was even restored as a council member in 1550.

Early in 1550, John Dudley, the earl of Warwick, emerged as the next leader of the council. Dudley had during the past year become increasingly popular because of his successes as a military leader, especially during Kett's Rebellion. However, he faced a lot of work to get the country back to a better and more united standpoint. England was in ruins. The government was in financial trouble. The people were completely divided, and whole cities had suffered at the hands of rioters. Dudley would ultimately be able to restore the reputation of the English government and get things running a little bit more smoothly. In the eyes of the nobility, he was seen as less arrogant than Seymour because he tended to involve his council members as well as the king in the decision making. While Seymour had treated Edward like a child, Dudley's manner was more respectful and focused on preparing the king for his future as the sole ruler of England.

As Dudley was solidifying his spot as the leader of the council, Edward was getting older and understanding more and more about the workings of the government. It is not definitely known when the young king started making decisions for his kingdom, but there are records that suggest he had some say on issues starting in his early teens. When Edward was 14 years old, he handpicked men to be members of a special "Counsel for the Estate." The group, which gathered for a meeting every week, briefed the king on all things that were considered to be of high importance. He also had a close working relationship with the two secretaries of state, William Petre and William Cecil.

When Dudley took over the reins of the privy council from Seymour, he chose not to assume the title of lord protector. Dudley, who was made duke of Northumberland in 1551, led the council in a much different manner than his predecessor had. In contrast to Seymour, he referred to the council members to try to get majority decisions, establishing the appearance of a good working government. However, it was not quite as righteous as it appeared. To stack the deck in his favor, Dudley added family members and supporters to the council, positions of power, and the king's household. In this way, he managed to rule the kingdom with less opposition.

While Seymour had led England into wars with other countries, Dudley tried to enact peace treaties with France and Scotland. He ordered the troops who were garrisoned in Boulogne and Scotland to come home and sought to ensure that England would not be spending any more money on wars; it was simply too expensive. Instead, Dudley beefed up the policing within England to combat any opposers of Edward's government and religious reforms. To further solidify England's new peaceful policy,

Edward was betrothed to Elisabeth of Valois, the daughter of the king of France, in 1551.

Keeping England out of costly wars was a good first step to rebuilding the economy, but peace alone would not be enough to get the country out of financial ruin. Dudley tried to improve the situation by debasing the coinage, but that just led to more problems. Finally, he entrusted the subject of finances to Thomas Gresham, an expert financier. By 1552, Gresham had turned the economy around, and England's trade was on the rise. There was more work to be done, but finally people saw the start of economic recovery in England.

In 1552, Edward Seymour, the duke of Somerset, would meet his demise. A few months earlier, Seymour had been arrested on charges of treason; he was suspected of conspiring against Dudley and the council to reclaim power over the kingdom for himself. Whether this was the case is not known for certain, but nevertheless Seymour was executed on January 22, 1552, after being convicted for having raised an army without a license. Seymour had generally been popular among the common people because of his public condemnation of the land enclosure policy, and his death led to many disliking his successor, Dudley.

Chapter Six

The English Reformation

"Dearest Mother, the only true consolation is from Heaven and the only real love is the love of God. Preserve, therefore, I pray you, my dear sister Mary from all the wiles and enchantments of the evil one, and beseech her to attend no longer to foreign dances and merriments which do not become a most Christian princess."

—Edward VI

The matter that Edward was most interested in during his reign was religion and the reformation of the Church of England. The first Protestant-born king, Edward wanted to continue the work that his father had started before him. He fully supported the break with Rome and the Catholic Church and wanted to spread Protestant practices of worship to all his subjects. On matters of religion, both Seymour and Dudley supported the beliefs of the young king and followed his policy. But the man Edward trusted more than anyone else when it came to religion was the archbishop of Canterbury, Thomas Cranmer. Cranmer was responsible for issuing the official religious reforms that would make the Church of England a fundamentally Protestant entity, rather than a Catholic Church that was separate from Rome.

It is important to note that there was financial gain to be made during the reformation even for non-believers. Confiscation of church property and dissolution of monasteries became a source of income for the Crown, and lands that had been previously owned by the church were sold to contented gentlemen or noblemen.

Although it's unclear whether Seymour, Dudley, or Edward's father Henry VIII truly were believing Protestants, Edward lived his life immersed in his religion. He read 12 chapters of scripture every day and often enjoyed sermons. Additionally, Edward staunchly believed that those still practicing Catholicism needed to convert. He could be quite tactless and overzealous in his approach to convince others of their need to follow the Protestant religion. For example, his relationship with his half-sister Mary rapidly declined because of her refusal to give up her Catholic belief. On the few occasions that the siblings met after Edward ascended to the throne, Edward would talk down to Mary even though she was 20 years his senior, openly condemning her for her choice of religion.

As a child, Edward had attended mass and participated in other Catholic rituals, but as he got older and was influenced by his Protestant tutors as well as Archbishop Cranmer he came to believe that Protestantism was the only true religion. Under Cranmer's guidance, Edward also became convinced that this true religion needed to be imposed on his people. Cranmer took it upon himself to assemble and issue a unified liturgy for the English people to follow since Edward was doing away with Roman Catholic rituals and practices. When his *Book of Common Prayer* was published in 1549, it was supposed to be a compromise and middle ground between what the traditionalists wanted from the reform and what the zealots desired. But it was met with a lot of opposition; neither side seemed pleased with the outcome. Two senior Catholic bishops, Stephen Gardiner and Edmund Bonner, were even arrested and sent to the Tower of London because of their criticisms of the *Book of Common Prayer*.

As the reformation moved along, Edward started taking on some of the responsibility that came with his position on the throne. After 1551, he started taking advantage of his role as the supreme head of the church. Edward was still influenced by many reformers, and he would sometimes take their notions and push their agendas if he saw value in them for the reforms.

In 1552, Cranmer issued a rewritten version of the *Book of Common Prayer* which was more concise and less ambiguous. It contained revisions to the canon law and the addition of the Forty-two Articles. The articles were meant to give people a clearer picture of what the practices of the reformed religion should look like, especially communion service which had previously been a point of contention. With the newly released *Book of Common Prayer*, mass was absolutely prohibited. The book was further backed up by the Act of Uniformity of 1552. For many, this was the year that the English Church truly became Protestant.

At last, everything seemed to be going well. The reformation was well on its way, the economy was recovering, all major rebellions had been quelled, and there was peace with France and Scotland. But this triumphant feeling would be short-lived. By the beginning of the

following year, it became evident that King Edward was
seriously ill.

Chapter Seven

Succession Crisis

"My devise for the succession…"

—Edward VI

In January of 1553, the king started showing signs of sickness. He developed a bad cough and fever. When his temperature rose to a pitch, he had severe chest pains and trouble breathing. It was not clear, at first, if his illness would take his life or not. Over the next few months, Edward would seem to get better at times but then relapse with high fever and relentless coughing. In May, doctors reported that the king was making a full recovery. But by the summer, it was clear that the king had worsened again, and he was likely not going to get better.

With Edward in such a perilous state, it was important to make preparations in case of his early death. The succession was set to be Mary as the next in line for the throne should the king pass away. Edward's half-sister, however, did not see eye-to-eye with him on the subject for which he cared most: religion. Mary's undying Catholic faith paired with her close relationship with Charles V, the Holy Roman Emperor, made it highly likely that England would reconnect with Rome should Mary ascend to the throne. Edward feared that if Mary took the throne, all he had done to advance the Protestant Church in England would be undone. Edward would not have that. He had to stop his sister.

Edward had strong support from his advisors in the matter of succession. Cranmer and Dudley did not want to see their work become obsolete and die along with the king. The council did not want to see Mary on the throne either. They feared for their seats and for their lives should she become the queen. Luckily, they were able to point to more than just religious differences to get Mary excluded from the line of succession. First, there was the question of Mary's legitimacy which stemmed from the time of her father's reign. Henry VIII had deemed both Mary and his other daughter Elizabeth illegitimate in his pursuit to annul the marriages to their mothers. Second, there had never been a female monarch in England who ruled in her own right. And since Mary was not married, if she took the throne, she would have to rule alone. All of those factors needed to be addressed with the naming of a different successor.

Edward ended up drafting a document entitled "My devise for the succession." The purpose of the document was to remove Mary and Elizabeth from the line of succession and officially name someone else. In the draft, Edward tried to name any future male heirs of the duchess of Suffolk, Frances Grey (the daughter of Mary Tudor). He also included male heirs of Margaret Clifford (the granddaughter of Mary Tudor). However, as neither Frances nor Margaret had any living male heirs, no existing person had been named as successor in this draft. Thus, there was no way to enforce this directive, so a second draft of the document had to be written.

With the help of his advisors and council members, Edward decided to name his cousin, Lady Jane Grey, who was 16 years old at the time. She was the eldest daughter of Frances Grey and was married to Dudley's son, Lord Guildford Dudley, since just a few weeks back. Lady Jane's grandmother was Mary Tudor and her great-grandfather Henry VII. Henry had been the first Tudor to serve as the king of England and Ireland and done so for about 24 years. Jane was smart and seen as one of the most educated and intelligent women of the time. But most importantly, Lady Jane and most of her family were Protestants. Even though Edward had failed to find a suitable male heir to succeed him, he was pleased that he would be passing the crown to someone who would continue the reformation work that he and his father had started.

In June, Edward asked to have the judges of the King's Bench brought to his chambers. He gave his document to the judges and told them to write an official, legal will based on what was in his "Devise." He also wanted those who would be enforcing his will to sign a bond in front of him that would require them to uphold the instructions in the will when the time came. The judges were taken aback by the king's orders. This situation had never presented itself before, so the judges were unsure of what to do. They took the document and left Edward's chambers to discuss how they were going to proceed.

English law held that no minor was allowed to make a will that would be legally enforceable. Edward was only 15 years old and, therefore, still a minor at the time. Also, the king was trying to bypass his father's Third Succession Act by excluding Mary and Elizabeth. With no precedent to refer to and based on the laws of England at that time, the judges decided to deny Edward's request. Dudley, whose son had married Lady Jane Grey, the would-be successor, was furious with the judges' refusal. He threatened them, saying he would fight any and all of them if they did not do as they were being told. He also started throwing around the word "treason" to intimidate them into cooperating.

The judges tried to negotiate different scenarios for the succession of the crown. One suggestion was to leave Mary in the line of succession but with the condition that she had to honor and continue Edward's reformation work. Dudley found that to be a ridiculous idea and simply laughed at it.

Frustrated, King Edward decided to speak to the judges again himself. He made it clear that they were to follow his orders, probably threatening charges of treason and punishment if they opposed. Finally, the lord chief justice gave in. In the end, over a hundred bishops, councilors, and sheriffs signed the king's "Devise." Dudley appears to have been instrumental in convincing his peers to approve Edward's will, which would make Dudley the future queen's father-in-law.

As June was drawing to a close and Edward was becoming increasingly frail, the English people became aware that their young king was inevitably going to die. Word was getting around—not only in England but other countries as well—that Mary was being removed from the line of succession. France, in particular, supported the king's wishes for Lady Jane Grey to succeed him. Because of France's many conflicts with the Holy Roman Empire, they did not want to see Charles V's cousin and ally, Mary, on the throne. The English people, on the other hand, supported Mary who they saw as the legitimate heir of Henry VIII. Nevertheless, Edward and the government were sure that they could successfully place Lady Jane on the throne.

With everything set in place with the will, Edward, and likely Dudley, wanted to ensure that the accession of Lady Jane would take place smoothly. Mary was at the time residing in her home at Hunsdon. King Edward sent her a summons to visit him in London before he died; it was supposed to be one last meeting between brother and sister. However, the truth was that Edward planned to have Mary captured and imprisoned so that she would not cause any trouble for Lady Jane's succession. Luckily, Mary was warned of her brother's intentions, and instead of going to London she traveled to East Anglia. Mary owned quite a few estates in the region, which was home to many supporters of the Roman Catholic faith. The area had been home to Kett's Rebellion, the uprising that Dudley had been instrumental in suppressing, so the people there would certainly rally behind Mary. Mary would remain in East Anglia until her brother died; it turned out that her wait for Edward's death would be a short one.

Chapter Eight

Death of a Boy King

"I am glad to die."

—Edward VI

In his final weeks, Edward's health declined quickly. He was coughing up blood and mucus, and his legs were so swollen that he became completely bedridden. On July 1, Edward managed to make an appearance from his window in Greenwich Palace. That short glimpse of their king gave the English people proof that Edward was close to death; the once tall and healthy young man had completely wasted away. Once word got around that Edward had been seen from his window, people started showing up outside the palace hoping to see the king. But he would not appear again. King Edward could not get up anymore; he was losing himself to the sickness that had settled in his body. He was too weak to go on. Shortly before he passed away, Edward reportedly told John Cheke, his tutor, "I am glad to die."

On July 6, 1553, King Edward VI died in his bed at Greenwich Palace. His last words were said to be, "I am faint; Lord have mercy upon me and take my spirit." The following month, Edward was buried at Westminster Abbey in the Henry VII Lady Chapel. Archbishop Thomas Cranmer performed the rituals. There was no marking added to the burial place at that time to indicate that Edward was laid to rest there. In 1966, a stone with an inscription was laid in the floor of the chapel by Christ's Hospital to honor Edward VI and the place where he was buried. The words of the inscription were, "In Memory of King Edward VI Buried In This Chapel This Stone Was Placed Here By Christ's Hospital In Thanksgiving For Their Founder 7 October 1966."

The cause of Edward's death has been debated throughout history and is not definitely known. There has been some speculation that the young king was poisoned, possibly by Dudley or by supporters of Mary. However, the doctor that performed Edward's autopsy claimed he found disease in his lungs. The cause of death was likely tuberculosis based on that report and Edward's symptoms.

Whatever the reason, the king was dead, and the throne was ripe for the taking. The struggle for power between the Protestants and the Catholics was about to ensue, and it was going to be a bloody battle.

Conclusion

Upon Edward's death, Dudley failed miserably in his attempt to instate Lady Jane as the next queen. By July 19, both Jane and Dudley were imprisoned in the Tower of London, and Mary was well on her way to becoming England's first queen regnant thanks to her massive popular support. Just as Edward had feared, it looked as if all of his work would become undone now that Mary had ascended to the throne.

Mary did try her hardest to reinstate Roman Catholicism as the main religion in England. She repealed many of Edward and Henry's religious laws and restored church doctrine to what it had been prior to Edward's rule. Mary would, however, face many obstacles on her journey to reverse the reformation. It proved hard to restore the church to what it had once been because so much land had been confiscated and sold to private landowners. And, with the revival of the Heresy Acts, Mary approved the burning of many prominent Protestants, for example Thomas Cranmer, which earned her the nickname "Bloody Mary." Mary's harsh persecution of dissenters made her unpopular with the people, and her decision to take a Spanish Catholic husband further deepened the rift with both her government and her people.

When Mary died in 1558, after only five years on the throne, she was succeeded by her half-sister Elizabeth. Elizabeth, who was Protestant, immediately set about continuing Edward and Henry's reformation of the church.

Under her rule, England would prosper and solidify many of Edward's religious reform into society.

Although Edward VI had a short life and only briefly reigned as king, he left a lasting impression, especially on the Church of England. Edward's reign was full of economic struggles and social unrest, but his work to advance the religious reformation of the Church of England changed the country forever. Edward VI claimed his place in history as the boy king who opened the doors for Protestantism and, eventually, other religions in England. Regardless of what happened after his death, one can still see the fruits of his labor present in the religious makeup of England today.

Made in United States
North Haven, CT
16 December 2021

12926339R00024